Blackbird

To Hope, sister poet

Laura Grace Weldon

Blackbird

poems

Laura Grace Weldon

GRAYSON BOOKS
West Hartford, CT
www.GraysonBooks.com

Library of Congress Control Number: 2018966660
ISBN: 978-0-9994327-6-1

interior & cover designs by Cindy Mercier
cover artwork by Bethany Bash

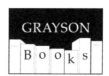

dedicated with love to
Olivia Marie, Callum James, and Brianna Grace

∽

A portion of all book royalties will be donated to the Medina Raptor
Center, a non-profit center in Spencer, Ohio which rescues,
rehabilitates, and releases injured and orphaned birds.

Contents

Acknowlededgments

Blue Collar Review "Border Children on the News"

Canary "Compost Happens"

Fourth and Sycamore "Skiff at the Shore"

Great Lakes Review "Finally, Then"

Gyroscope Review "Bad Start," "Tsk From the Dead," and "Astral Chorus"

Holistic Parenting Magazine "Welcome"

Listen. A Seeker's Resource for Spiritual Direction "Common Ground"

Literary Mama "Survivors of Child Abuse Support Group"

Mom Egg Review "Failure Too"

Neurology: Journal of the American Academy of Neurology "Subdural Hematoma"

One: Jacar Press "Inside Out"

Peacock Journal "Overflowing"

Penman Review "Adjunct Accidentally Invited to the Club"

Poetry 24 "Divisions"

Pulse: Voices From the Heart of Medicine "Home Invasion"

Rise Up Review "Why Bottles Litter Interstate Hillsides"

Shot Glass Journal "Feral," "Fog as Visible Dreams," "Let's Turn Off the Porch Light," and "What the Onion Teaches"

Silver Birch Press "Summer Day at Huntington Beach"

The MOON Magazine "Anything, Everything," "November Morning at Dawn," "Post Hoc, Ergo Propter Hoc," "Weed I Won't Pull," and "What It Carries, Still"

Typehouse "Temporal Reminders on I-480," "Moving Day"

Verse-Virtual "Fine Furniture"

Writers Resist "Clarion Reminder"

Writing for Peace "Earthbound"

Earthbound

Are we supposed to settle for a planet
lagging behind our expectations?
We want reversible time,
admission into past or future
easy as changing our minds.
We want teleportation, so we can
zip anywhere for the afternoon,
maybe Iceland or Argentina,
where we'll make new friends,
agree to meet up for lunch
next week in Greece
on only an hour's break.

We want to get past
greed and suffering and war,
enough already.
And death? That's awfully primitive
for souls with so much left to learn.

That said, this planet does a lot right.
Birds, for one.
Water in all its perfect manifestations.
Those alive poems called trees.
The way a moment's glance
can reveal a kindred spirit.

Which we all are, really.
The oneness between self and everything
is this planet's secret, kept imperfectly.
That's more than we might expect.
Although time travel would be nice.

Galloping Rap Smack Thwack

You and I get maybe two billion some beats
before our hearts give out. Our inner drums thump
in polyrhythm with heartbeats of people walking by,
of birds overhead, of dogs snuffling at our feet.
Each pulsation joins a planet-wide syncopation,
our thrumming hearts a percussion section
to the consonance and dissonance
here on Earth.

Sometimes mine is a wild horse, skittish,
a galloping rap, smack, thwack in the cage of my chest.
If tachycardic beats subtract seconds,
I want to savor time.
Let's not bother with small talk.
Let's let our minutes linger longer
as we tell each other every one of our stories.

What the Onion Teaches

Anything, seen wholly,
teaches everything.
Take a raw onion, harsh to its core.
Unpeel, un-ring, and hold to the light.
It is complete as the soil, sun, and rain
of its making.

Sauté the rings in oil
till the onion relaxes into itself,
elevating everything added next.

This looking, this warmth and trust,
is how the prisoner finds Shakespeare,
the lonely child discovers trees,
the battered woman pulls away layers
ready to be seen.

House on Smith Road

Built on a swollen lip of land
where railroad tracks curve out of sight,
the house barely stands.
Behind it, what once was a barn
rests in an exhale of timber.
Battered cars cluster close,
rusty flies drawn to decay.
Painted plywood band-aided
to the side, blue tarp tacked on the roof.

It's someone's home.
Every time I drive by
I'm relieved to see light in a window,
laundry flapping defiantly on the line,
faded red plastic flowers
potted on the porch.
No matter what's done to her,
or undone too long,
this hunched great-grandmother
shelters her family.

One day a sign appears, jaunty colors
out of place in that ragged yard.
Soon, mail no longer bulges
in the bent roadside box.
Cars are towed.
Within weeks
the tarp twists away,
part of the roof caves in,
the porch buckles.

There are people who keep going
past all predictions,
chewed up by cancer
or rattling with emphysema.
They hold things together
for the daughter struggling
with heroin, the spouse
wandering through dementia.

I think of them as this house
slides ever closer to the ground,
plastic flowers still blooming
on that brave tilting porch.

Clarion Reminder

The powerful provoke the powerless
to push against one another.
Their power grows by keeping us
in all kinds of prisons.

Yet we are not powerless.

Remember the black bear
roaming Clarion County, Pennsylvania,
its head trapped a month or more
in a metal-ringed pail.

Remember those who chased it for hours,
grabbed it in a perilous embrace,
carefully sawed loose those tight bonds.

Imagine what they felt as the bear
ran free into the woods.

Imagine too, the bear.

Abbreviation Nation

I write full state names on packages and letters.
Squinch them into tiny postal declaration forms.
My pen describes the undulating topography of
Wyoming,
West Virginia,
Oklahoma,
Montana.

So much lost when states are known
by capital letters, ugly as grades
scrawled on a fifth grader's report
about Utah's gross domestic products,
when that girl wants instead
to study mountain lions, take
into herself their sleek ease,
alert on a branch, unseen.

Consider places known by waters,
the way their appellations flow
into us as we speak them.
Alaska asks lips to move in waves
like the Aleut expression meaning
"that which the sea breaks against."

Connecticut tap dances the tongue,
hints at the Algonquian name
Quinnehtukqut
for "beside the long tidal river."
Minnesota comes from the Dakota word
for "sky-tinted water"
and Ohio from the Iroquois word
ohi-yo' meaning "great river."

Perhaps the name Idaho,
cheery to pronounce
as a settler's invitation to dance,
is most quintessentially American
in that it's an invented word,
meaning unknown.

Why Bottles Litter Interstate Hillsides

On a steep slope behind a wire fence
meant to keep deer off the road,
suburban boys gather. Each brings
microbrews found in upscale fridges
or energy drinks sloshed with vodka.
They lean away from the ground's tilt.
Drink, brag, smoke, jeer, jostle for position.

The highway courses endlessly below them,
overpasses and underpasses heading six directions,
every vehicle steering away.
Traffic noise fills the night, fills their bodies,
amps up a signature restlessness.
In earlier eras, boys their age claimed
homesteads, climbed ship rigging,
set type, shaped glass, forged iron.
Instead they're here on this cold night.
Words steam and fade
into exhaust-heavy air.

Every day in every boy's memory,
they've been graded on doing
a backpackful of nothing.
Here they snap saplings, toss bottles,
sometimes hoist the drunkest kid
halfway over the fence. They're told
you've got your whole life ahead of you
but wonder, unspoken, how they'll ever
merge onto lanes taking them there.

Call of the Void

Safe behind a 20-story window
or buckled in around mountain curves,
terror still hatchets your viscera,
tosses an ice pick in your logic.
But this terror tingles with attraction.

It whispers "jump" at the edge
of a subway platform,
urges you to twist the wheel
toward a sheer drop, tempts you
to open the plane's door
at 35,000 feet. No,
you don't want to die.

Experts call it High Place Phenomenon,
a temporary uncoupling of perceptual systems,
although science can't possibly describe
what you feel. In France it's known
as *l'appel du vide* or "call of the void."

Every cell of your being responds
to that call, every cell
wavers at the brink.
Seconds stretch
out of proportion
till you shudder from the trance,
allow the abyss in you
to step back from the void.

Temporal Reminders on I-480

Raccoon beside the road
is puffed in death to the roundness
of a child's toy;
belly curved, paws up.
An electronic zither of flies
shape-shifting this breathless form into
breath of carbon dioxide and water vapor,
into *spiritus*.

Bacteria, blowflies, beetles,
and wasps engage
in divine, perfect work
while the tail's striped fur
ripples in the breeze.

Ahead a silver pickup swerves
into another lane, honks,
brake checks the car behind.

Finally, Then

After dinner is over, dishes clean,
their porcelain lips stacked in smiles
behind the cupboard door.

After your desk is organized,
emails sent, final draft finished,
your to-do list a flock of check marks
like migratory birds flapping
down the column and out
to the horizon of a light-suffused land
called Everything is Done.

Finally, you can do whatever it is
you say you've always wanted to do.
Or not said, because naming can sometimes
dilute a dream's dark essence.

But there's a bank overdraft to fix,
unread library books to return,
another doctor's appointment,
and these days when you accelerate,
your car makes a screaming noise
like a small trapped animal.
You can picture its curled body
and dark eyes, terrified your speed
will toss it onto the moving parts
of a machine made only to go go go.

Maybe, after you get the car fixed,
clear up a few other things,
finally, then, you'll have time.

Adjunct Accidentally Invited to the Club

Air is soft here
fluffed silk against skin,
each seam lying just so.
Here the heft
of a Yale ring,
shoes that must be Italian,
a wristwatch pricier
than two years of her wages.

Frayed cuffs turned under
a decades-old shirt,
cheap even when new,
mark her a smiling interloper
though no one seems
to see her at all.

Faces here are smooth,
postures casual,
mergers and acquisitions
mentioned lightly.
Laughter puddles
gem-like around conversations.
She imagines herself an anthropologist
coding this privileged tribe.

Barely touched trays of opulent food
swing back to the kitchen
in the arms of tuxedoed waiters.
She wants to hide those leftovers
in her cold car. Drive home.
Fill the refrigerator
in the house where she hopes
the roof stops leaking,
the jacket with a broken zipper
makes it through another winter.

She doesn't. Smiles instead,
head tipped to the side, as if included
in a conversation on her right.
Visiting the bathroom before leaving,
one so deluxe it has an anteroom

with damask couches,
she slips a heavy bar of milled soap
into her purse. Its weight
a scant measure of how much
they've already taken.

Fine Furniture

Maybe it was the car we parked outside,
poxed with rust, shaped like a bar of soap.
Maybe it was our worn clothes, scuffed shoes.
Maybe it was my mother-in-law,
deferential as a servant.
Maybe it was my husband. Maybe me.

My mother-in-law now lived with us,
so we browsed for lamp-shaped optimism
in her favorite shade of blue.
The owner approached,
hair perfect, clothes elegant
on the hanger of her shoulders.
"You probably won't find
what you're looking for here,"
she said, face mannequin blank.
"Might I suggest another store?"

Today that shop's windows are slapped
with Going Out of Business signs.
I let sympathy shake my head,
imagine the owner now knows
money isn't sturdy as furniture,
isn't alive as a tree.
Wealth knows less than
this breeze. I hear it
whisper *winter, winter*,
through gumdrop green leaves.

Divisions

Our pear tree is hardly taller than I am,
branches bent with ripe fruit
mottled gold and brown.
Each pear plucked
is a welcome
weight in the hand,
in the basket. Even
rotting fruit at my feet
is a celebration of hornets.
I think of these pears
in the mouths of children I love.
I squint at neighbors' homes,
recently shadowed by Trump signs,
want to offer this sweetness to them all,
want to ask blessings to settle over every one of us.
Instead I carry the pears inside. This division is on me, too.

Let's Turn Off the Porch Light

Dappled brown moths
woolly as Grammy's needlepoint
whirl around the bulb,
winged pilgrims desperate
for union with the Holy.

Little suns everywhere
lure us to the surface of things
where we burn for lack of shadows,
mistaking the blaze of want
for a larger love.

Home Invasion

Get out my green mug, round as a pregnant belly.
Casually pour grounds in the filter
despite monitoring devices warning
of an intruder's presence.
Act normally. Breathe deeply.

Let the cosmic swirl of cream in hot coffee
remind me how small one lifetime is
in an infinite universe. Remember
the Vedas say God's playfulness is expressed
through perpetual creation and destruction.

Quell fear. Be peace.
Ignore creaks and groans as intruder
inches closer. Pretend
the future is a given,
as it was before
the diagnosis.

Notice to Fibromuscular Dysplasia

Loathe to accept my own diagnosis, I do.
Appreciate more moments,
slather gratitude more thickly,
though that's long been my schtick.
Not enough?
Okay, you blood whirling disease, I'll amp it up.
Offer you my strength, my aspirations.
But don't for one fucking second think you can touch my child.
I will call down every power held in abeyance until now.
I've met obstacles with love,
or as much love as I could summon.
I've smiled, understood, cared down to my marrow.
Turned the other cheek. Turned another. And another.
Given more cheeks than God put in layaway.
This does not extend to my girl,
sick from babyhood when ease should be given.
You will not touch her now,
not another slap of vertigo,
not another punch of hemiplegia.
I am a tornado, earthquake, tsunami.
I will knock your house into splinters.
I will drown you in my tides.
I will drop you into a fissure so deep
you won't hear yourself cry for mercy.
I am the will of every mother
in every eon's arduous crawl from sea to land.
You cannot have my child.
Come here. Take me.
But leave my daughter alone.

Fog As Visible Dreams

Mysteries flicker under each tender eyelid.
Become mist. Pass through walls.
Crowd the street, stories in symbol
lingering over a neighborhood asleep.

Houses and mailboxes
move toward my headlights,
ghosts stepping into form.
I see each thing clearly
only as it passes by.

Moving Day

The new people don't yet know
this knuckled lawn glistens
with tiny flowers each spring,
an acre of white slung like a scarf
over the horizon's curved shoulder.

They haven't seen autumn here,
skies dark yet bright. Trees
clothed in crimson and coral
more vivid than any stained glass window.
Even passing cars are cast in a cathedral glow.

The new people don't know
we tucked blessings behind these walls.
On bare beams the kids crayoned
bubble-face stick figures
and I wrote poems
in thick black marker, dizzied
by vapors that make words permanent.

Dust from our skin waits
on light fixtures, door frames,
and carpets. It will lift into motes,
enter their bodies as they breathe.
On each surface our fingerprints linger.
They are too light to pack
too heavy to carry.

Welcome

Eyes, fingertips, tongues
form one from two.
Yield three.

You.

Snowflake fingerprints,
tiny palms creased with foreknowledge,
DNA whirling proteins
into the plot of a new story.

Despite vast mathematical improbabilities
here you are.
Your mother's hundred thousand eggs
your father's five trillion sperm,
a one-in-five-hundred-million-million-million
chance of your existence.

Our gladness is incalculable.

How To Soothe

When babies cried
my father picked them up,
politely, as if to apologize
for their locomotion issues,
then stepped outside.
He named trees, birds, rain.
"This is grass," he'd say.
"In no time at all
you'll be running on it."
Babies calmed at once,
eyes wide, awake
to the planet's glories.

I learned from my father
it's a matter of walking
inside to out
with someone capable
of truly seeing.

Survivors of Child Abuse Support Group

Tuesday evenings I can't think of my baby
or the current between us
more elemental than love,
switches my milk on,
wetting the shirt
under my buttoned blazer.
My job is to listen
as people unknot the past.

The guy who constantly flirts,
his smile sugar white,
admits to road rage. Others
laugh in recognition,
their cars monsters too.

A young mother,
chandelier of dreads shaking,
mocks overheard endearments
like "Precious" and "Sweetie Pie,"
the same names I call my baby.

An older woman, beautiful
and resolutely friendless, agrees.
Affection shown children in public
sickens her. At home
kids are tied in the attic
or locked in a dog cage.
She knows this for sure.

Then Wilson speaks up,
says he feels good.
He's taken his stove apart,
cleaned filth under and behind.
Wilson's father dragged him from bed
to scrub for hours, sometimes his tongue
the rag. Or dragged him to the basement
to menace more than his tongue.

Empathy rises from Wilson
freely as other people sweat.
He and his wife cared for foster children

from the time their own sons were small.
Wilson kept the house clean,
took them to church, taught them the secret
of balancing a two-wheeler,
but his sons became angry strangers.
Since the divorce they don't speak to him at all.

He now knows
through all those years of dinner together
and homework done neatly,
older boys carrying hurt too large to contain
tormented his children in their own beds.
Wilson, his hands raw from scrubbing,
smiles as he says softly,
The stove is spotless.
Everyone in the circle of folding chairs
nods, understanding.

Border Children in the News

Frantic families send their children
past drug runners and thieves,
through deserts, on tops of freight trains,
over 1,700 miles seeking
refuge at our border.

Tonight, we tweeze sushi into our mouths
under a blast of chilled Happy Hour air.
Screens broadcast dark-eyed children
behind chain link fences
while protestors chant
go back home! and *U-S-A!*

A congressman vows to expedite
their return to *where they belong*.
"Yeah, deprived of a hearing," we mutter
and a guy eating spicy duck wings
next to us says "there are laws for a reason."

Agile in conflict studies,
the bartender sets out
complimentary edamame.
Offers refills.
Changes the TV station.
Lets the comprehensible violence
of hockey soothe
as our drinks arrive.

Subdural Hematoma

Thank you Dr. Gandhivarma Subramaniam

Squeezed into pain's tight grip,
my son finally agrees to an ER visit, where
images of his brain's convoluted architecture
show it pushed aside
by blood's gleaming fist.

Seated in waiting room furniture
thickly layered with other people's prayers,
we pass time knuckled and blank
while neurosurgeons saw open his skull.

I think of the girl who fell
10,000 feet from a broken plane
into Peru's jungle. Tightly clustered trees
cushioned her, their limbs breaking
to set her on the forest floor
still safely strapped in her seat.
Wearing white sandals and a frilly dress
she walked along a stream 11 days
to find rescuers. At first, those men
feared she might be a river ghost.

I want to strap my own son in
so miraculous a seat.
Drop him in a current
where time rushes backward,
before a guy late for his shift
at a donut shop
makes an illegal left turn,
before my son's helmet hits the car,
before my son's body
skids down the pavement,
before vessels begin leaking
into the dear familiar head
I first glimpsed in the birthing room.

Benjamin wakes, blue eyes watery
against ghostly pale skin,
map of a dark river
etched deep across his forehead.

He turns to us, jesting
"No drain bramage!"
to let us know
he's out of the jungle.

Weed I Won't Pull

Some hardship curved it into
a green ampersand. Tendrils sprout
along a resolute stem.

I want to lean close, ask
for some photoautotrophic wisdom.

Listen to the soil's bacterial choir.

Convert to the worship
plants have practiced since the Beginning.

Post Hoc, Ergo Propter Hoc

With a twitch of her nose, Samantha could
halt sickness, visit other realms, reverse time.
Instead she chose to pass as a mortal housewife
folding laundry, planning dinner parties.
At nine, I saw better uses for her powers,
fervently twitched my nose, yet couldn't
end the war in Vietnam, couldn't even
read blurry assignments on the blackboard.

Now I'm nine times six, and if I could
I'd cast a spell over this planet.
Greed would be erased, stories heard,
courage shared, wildness celebrated,
love revealed as the real magic.
Wishing hasn't made this happen.

Yet since *Bewitched* began,
baby girls have been named Samantha
more than any time in history.
No nose twitches reported,
but Earth sees more girls educated, more
women elected, more laws respecting our rights.
Summoning *will*, that's what women called witches
have always used to birth a better reality.
Today they are everywhere. They pass as your sister,
your mother-in-law, your Facebook friend,
your own glorious self.

How to Play Blackbird

Think of a question.
Speak it aloud.
Then splay a dictionary open, preferably a hefty one
with lettered indentations along the side
and tiny exacting illustrations of insects and theorems.
Without looking, place your finger on the page
and read whatever definition you touch.
The answer is code you must unravel.

"Why is my hair curly?" my child asks.
Eyes shuttered, his fingernail plops onto *law*.
First definition, *binding force or effect*.
Second definition, *regularity in natural occurrences*.
Genetic determinants, Blackbird caws.

I ask if I am strong enough,
then open and drop my finger on *panoply*.
First definition, *a complete or magnificent array*.
Second definition, *a complete suit of armor*.
Strength courses through my cells.

Know this.
Every dictionary holds more than definitions.
It contains an oracle,
wings folded, patient,
waiting to speak.

Failure Too

Failure is more than shame's
hot tar and feathers.

It is cancer cells
destroyed daily
in the body's
relentless furnace.

An unseen mugger
turning away
as a friend's greeting
crosses the street, bright
streamers through the dark.

The beads of a broken necklace
rolling in his mother's
dresser drawer, evidence
of that long-gone afternoon
he scooped blue stones and dust
from the floorboards,
weeping till she soothed
with words softer
than her disappointment.

Finding them the week she died
he's glad the necklace broke,
carries those stones
in his pocket to this day,
as ruins remind
us of splendor
in civilizations that spawned us.

Assembly Required

I just need a new body
my mother used to say,
as if she could unscrew her head,
fasten it to an updated version
without shortness of breath,
swollen legs, pain-weighted pulse.
We'd laugh about body shopping,
maybe at a superstore
offering various models.
This one with robotic joints
for creak-free reliability,
that one with an unbreakable heart.
We'd chortle about the likelihood
of a discount on her trade-in
but she'd grow thoughtful,
saying, *I'd still be me, just newer.*

She wished for a new body so often
I forgot it was a disguise,
rubber nose and curled moustache
worn over the longing to live well,
live longer.
One time I joked,
You're really talking
reincarnation, Mom.
She never brought it up after that
and I wanted to take my words back,
let us go on imagining replacement bodies
good at ballroom dancing, skiing, hang gliding.
Bodies with adjustable ages.
Bodies with wings, with second sight.

Compost Happens

Nature teaches nothing is lost.
It's transmuted.

Spread between rows of beans,
last year's rusty leaves tamp down weeds.
Coffee grounds and banana peels
foster rose blooms. Bread crumbs
scattered for birds become song.
Leftovers offered to chickens come back
as eggs, yolks sunrise orange.
Broccoli stems and bruised apples
fed to cows return as milk steaming in the pail,
as patties steaming in the pasture.

Surely our shame and sorrow
also return,
composted by years
into something generative as wisdom.

This German Shepherd

Who he was lingers with us,
his fear of water, love of cats,
his tail swish, glad sniff,
tired *garumphf* at the day's close.

In his thirteenth year, this good dog
walked with me despite
the disease that would take him.
One bright day he yanked me into a ditch
as a truck hurtled past.
The driver braked hard, backed up, blamed
sun in his eyes, said the dog saved me.

I know there are greater sorrows,
still, a shock of grief shook loose
when Jedi Moon had to be put down.

While reading on the couch,
I sometimes let one hand dangle
to rest on the memory of his vigilant spine.

Overflow

Full names bestowed at birth are announced
as the capped and gowned cross the stage.
I'm teary for the first student,
still verklempt 390 graduates later
when the bright light I call my son
shakes the dean's hand.

In his final years my father's eyes
filled at a tender story or fond memory.
In his last minute, tears issued
a farewell he couldn't utter.

The older I get, the more my reservoir
spills over at a science journal's
wonder-dense words,
a remembered song, an Instagram photo.

Soon I'll drip
like the icons of St. Mark Coptic church.
Not miraculous tears, just the world's beauty
overflowing, like every other member
of the Sacred Order of the Lachrymose,

prepared to daub my eyes
even at a baby's
peek-a-boo in the grocery store.
Her thick fingers clutching an apple,
me pared down to the core.

Tsk from the Dead

I shouldn't stack dishes in Jenga piles
but our cupboards are crowded from keeping
what our mothers and grandmothers used.
I use them too, hoping the blue milk pitcher
and cut glass butter dish take up space
in newly forming memories,
though neither the people we love
nor the things they cherished last long enough.

This afternoon I break the lid of a Corning Ware
casserole older than I am. As it shatters,
I swear a long-dead relative *tsks*
behind and slightly above my left shoulder.
I hear disappointment
weighted by all that dish held

until I realize it's an ironic *tsk*,
from a far more cosmic viewpoint.
One that knows
antique clocks kept in working condition,
documents stored on the cloud,
and 10,000 daily steps
can't keep us from losing everything
in our short spangling acceleration
from birth to whatever waits after death.

Her *tsk* implies the afterlife is lit
by awe, a transitory wattage here.
It shimmers in a stranger's hand
reaching out to stop a fall,
in a smile unfurling on a face
long closed with grief,
in the startling wonder of hearing
the dead *tsk* when we break a dish.

Your Test Results

I will unfold and smooth out
every crumpled scrap of luck
ever offered to me.
Set out traps
baited sweet with distraction
to catch stray unnoticed minutes.
Fling a net skyward,
to gather every wish ever wished
for your happiness.
I will shrink myself smaller
than your lymphocytes,
sneak into a pore,
bargain with the tiny gods
running the body
that houses your soul
until your test results transform
into the language angels speak.
I hear them now.
By phone or text
or MyChart message
they sing
this holy word:
normal.

Common Ground

What's incomplete in me seeks refuge
in blackberry bramble and beech trees,
where creatures live without dogma
and water moves in patterns
more ancient than philosophy.
I stand still, child eavesdropping on her elders.
I don't speak the language
but my body translates as best it can,
wakening skin and gut, summoning
the long kinship we share with everything.

Beyond Pasture Gates

It came for Isabelle while she
stood on 17-year-old hooves,
nibbling purple clover.
It came as a red halter led
her beyond pasture gates,
near a deep brown womb
dug in the green,
the same land she'd drawn from
to make milk we turned into cheese, yogurt, butter,
the same land she'd drawn from to make calves,
knitting bone, breath, blinking lashes
out of all this green.

With no more notice than she'd give a fly,
she took the vet's syringe, slowly settling
on the grass where she slept, then died.

~ ~ ~

In summer's shimmering heat the men of my family
release wire's long-held tension, coil fencing,
wrest thick round posts from the ground one by one.
Tall grasses remain, bent into wind's whirling cursive.
No cattle stand in these fields, the barn is empty,
leaving only what green remembers
now that the cows have come home.

November Morning at Dawn

Jacket over nightgown over boots
I walk out back exhaling clouds,
bucket of kitchen scraps swinging in hand.

Better than a ticket to Severance Hall
this shattery crunch of footfalls on frost,
wind-whirled barn vent trilling soprano,
high-tension wires humming baritone.

Inside the hay-muted hush
I lift a rusty handle, trusting water
will rush to my command,
trusting my arms to lift
this brimming pail.

I carry so many disappointments.
Little chance now to do more
than a scrap of what I meant to do
in this unadorned life.

Still, I sing with wind-tossed trees
and talk to creatures,
those I feed
and those I hope find food
through the cold of this coming winter.

Tonight, next to my beloved,
I'll drift to sleep slowly
listening to coyote songs.

I never expected peace
to soothe my scuffed mind
and yet it does. Sometimes
I bake too much bread, just so
there's more to carry out back
as an offering.

After Play

Beads puddled in a plastic bowl,
wooden whale's string tangled
with wind-up doll and turtle wheels.
Library books stacked like wealth,
summoning mouth's memory of words
read aloud, lap's memory of a child's
warm weight anchored by stories.
There's more to it than picking up
today's diorama. I want to hold
this time and yet fling myself forward.

In one damp discarded sock
and one sticky sippie cup
these children's cells
speak of their mandate to grow
up, away, beyond my lifetime.
If I squint I see the future
hurtle past with comet speed.
Look, there in the corner,
meteor showers sparkle
from a pile of puzzle pieces.

Skiff at the Shore

If only you could prepare a handy satchel.
Tuck in coffee's taste, thunder's smell,
sound of wind in autumn leaves, plus
your children's faces, such beloved faces.
And hugs, blessed hugs, even if you have to
take out books to fit every hug inside.

At night, wakeful, you ask yourself if pale yellow stars
sparking inside your eyes are a dream
or your brain's essence blinking out.
You haven't packed, can't seem to find a bag.
Have no map.

When are they coming back
your three-year-old granddaughter asks
about cows no longer in the barn,
about the cat buried by the fencepost,
about withered plants crumbling back to dirt.

You're told a skiff waits at your shore.
Ninety or more years from now
she'll board it herself,
arrive to find the table set,
Sunday dinner ready,
everyone back together.

What It Carries, Still

Your father, whose voice scared me,
whose head loomed a full 14 inches over mine,
bought us our only housewarming gift;
a bright blue, six cubic foot wheelbarrow.
We laughed at its size, laughed as you gave me
a bumpy ride over the first lawn
we giddily called our own.

He seemed to believe our future
would be one of Paul Bunyan-sized loads.
It was.

In it we hauled firewood, dirt, rocks,
crinkled leaves topped with squealing toddlers.
It held a big block Dodge engine.
It toted rolls of fencing, chicken feed, cow manure.
It carried trays of tender seedlings
out to the garden, waiting
as I blessed each one into soft earthen beds.

Today you mend the rusted body
of our battered blue wheelbarrow.
I wish your father lived to see
its wooden handles smoothed from use
and what it carries, still
on that one sure wheel.

Gone Gray

Your hair, once Viking red-blonde
is gray as dove feathers,
as a wolf pelt. While you sleep
I curve to keep close the scent of your skin.
The window frames us in moonlight.
May the peace we've finally found
linger in the drawer
of our descendants' DNA.

Summer Day at Huntington Beach

I tick with alarm clock worry.
My sister is afraid of nothing.
Not the dark or death or
Jay Preslan down the street
who pushes kids in front of cars.

Look at her run into the water
while I stand squinting.
She doesn't pinch her nose
to dive under. Doesn't pause
before splashing back
strange splashing kids. Doesn't heed
the lifeguard's megaphoned warning
to stay away from the ropes.

Lake Erie grabs at the shore,
slurps it greedily in foaming waves.
I picture monstrous goggly-eyed fish
lurking under the pier,
ships skudding in the depths,
lost sailors forever unburied.
I inhale the curved scent
of suntan lotion, clench my toes
in the sand, stand still. Far out,
bobbing in foil-bright waves,
my sister is another being entirely,
straining at the boundary ropes
trying to see all the way to Canada.

Inside Out

Only by snapping open scarlet runner bean pods
do we see they are lined with fuzz, shaped
to each vividly hued bean
like a viola case to its instrument.

Only by slicing open a trout
are its bones revealed, lined up like pews
facing the back of a moving church,
its scripture stories of what came before.

We see stars only in the darkness,
feed a flame only by burning.
fuel our bodies only with what lived.
You'd think we'd see a pattern,

yet are surprised when loss
tilts our world, lifestream
into waterfall. We're told grief
ebbs, when all we want to do

is bring sorrow's fullness
out in the sun's cleansing light.
Lay it on the rocks.
Let it air.

Bad Start

to the day, what with finding
feathers, then bodies
of two hens killed by hawks.
And power out, so I can't
work despite glaring deadlines.

Picking tomatoes and chard
for breakfast, I step on a bee
whose final act is to heave
her brave sword in my sole.
Startled, I skid on dew-wet grass,
fall sharply, my face whirling
a breath's distance from roses
prickled with scarifying thorns,

and laugh.

I'd been soggy
cereal in the bowl,
mail dropped in a ditch,
a garden wizened by blight,

but now,
foot in lap, I pinch
out the stinger,
stabbed by gratitude
for an insect's
venomous antidote.
Now all I see is a shining
curtain of light pulled open
to the third act of a comedy
performed as it
is lived.

Feral

Moonlight leaks through the curtains.
I lie awake, listen to coyote songs
circle and connect, stitching together
the night's raw edges.

Each time I hear their howls
my bone marrow sings.
What's muzzled in me lifts.
I seem silent and still,
yet my pulse races through the trees.

Astral Chorus

"Stars resonate like a huge musical instrument."
—Bill Chaplin, asteroseismologist

Late for chores after dinner with friends,
I walk up the darkening path,
my mind knitting something warm
out of the evening's words.
The woods are more shadow
than trees, barn a hulking shape on its slope.
I breathe in autumn's leaf-worn air, aware
I am glad to be in this place, this life.
The chickens have come in
from their wanderings. Lined up
like a choir, they croon soft lullabies.
A flock of stars stirs a navy-blue sky.
I can't hear them, but I'm told they
sing of things we have yet to learn.

Anything, Everything

"Find everything you're looking for?" a clerk asks
and I say, "I'm still looking for world peace."
"Can I get you anything else?" a nurse asks
and I say, "Yes, a safe haven for refugees."
For a millisecond, their faces soften
as they take a deep breath of imagining
then laugh or shake their heads
or commiserate. For a few minutes
we might even discuss
our planet's highest possibilities.
Maybe that deep breath,
that imagining,
is a starting place.

Notes on the Poems

Astral Chorus: Research on KIC 11026764, a star about 3,100 trillion miles from Earth, indicates that stars vibrate with a "harmonic hum" due to starquakes resonating from core to surface.

Call of the Void: *The Journal of Affective Disorders* reports on this syndrome in an article titled "An urge to jump affirms the urge to live: an empirical examination of the high place phenomenon."

Clarion Reminder: The young bear, its head trapped inside a bag normally used to cushion tractor trailers, was freed on Labor Day 2014.

Overflow: Pope Shenouda III, 117th Pope of Alexandria & Patriarch of the See, declared tears seeping from icons of St. Mark Coptic Orthodox Church in Cleveland, Ohio to be an official miracle.

Subdural Hematoma: In 1971, Juliane Koepcke was a passenger of an airliner that broke up mid-air after a lightening strike. She was the sole survivor.

About the Author

Laura Grace Weldon is the author of a previous poetry collection titled *Tending* and a handbook of alternative education called *Free Range Learning*. She works as a book editor and lives with vast optimism on a small farm where she'd get more done if she didn't spend so much time reading library books, cooking weird things, and singing to livestock. Connect with her at lauragraceweldon.com.

CPSIA information can be obtained
at www.ICGtesting.com
Printed in the USA
FFHW020729150319
50970465-56442FF